WELCOME TO THE 2019 MANCHESTER UNITED ANNUAL!

Think you know everything about United? Hopefully we can teach you even more about your favourite club.

As well as telling you all about the Reds' first team squad and providing loads of trivia about them, we introduce Casey Stoney and the newly-formed Manchester United Women.

We celebrate the evolution of David De Gea into the world's best goalkeeper, while also looking closer to home at the club's famous Academy. Graduates tell us what it's like to come up through the Reds' ranks, and what look at the local lads would be complete without a rundown of Jesse Lingard's finest celebrations to date?

There's all of this and more besides in the 2019 Manchester United Annual. Once we've finished dishing out the facts, you can test your Reds knowledge and, if you know your history, you could win a United shirt signed by first team squad members!

Read on, enjoy, and keep the Red flag flying high…

PLAYER PROFILES

2018/19 PREMIER LEAGUE SQUAD LIST

1. DAVID DE GEA
2. VICTOR LINDELOF
3. ERIC BAILLY
4. PHIL JONES
6. PAUL POGBA
7. ALEXIS SANCHEZ
8. JUAN MATA
9. ROMELU LUKAKU
10. MARCUS RASHFORD
11. ANTHONY MARTIAL
12. CHRIS SMALLING
13. LEE GRANT
14. JESSE LINGARD
15 ANDREAS PEREIRA
16. MARCOS ROJO
17. FRED

18. ASHLEY YOUNG
20. DIOGO DALOT
21. ANDER HERRERA
22. SERGIO ROMERO
23. LUKE SHAW
25. ANTONIO VALENCIA
27. MAROUANE FELLAINI
31. NEMANJA MATIC
36. MATTEO DARMIAN
39. SCOTT MCTOMINAY
44. TAHITH CHONG
46. JOSHUA BOHUI
47. ANGEL GOMES
48. ETHAN HAMILTON
51. MATEJ KOVAR

POSITION: GOALKEEPER

1

"The most important thing is to help the team in every way you can and to maintain consistency; I believe that's what makes the difference."

DAVID
DE GEA

"Maybe once there was a debate about whether he was the best goalkeeper in the world or not, but I don't think there's any question now."

PHIL JONES

BORN: 7 NOVEMBER 1990; MADRID, SPAIN

When David De Gea joined United in 2011, no goalkeeper had ever won the club's player of the year award. In 2017/18 he won it for the fourth time – more than any other player. The Spaniard's crazy reflexes and calm head are the keys to his success.

UNITED HONOURS (SO FAR)

- Premier League ✓
- Europa League ✓
- FA Cup ✓
- League Cup ✓
- Community Shield ✓ ✓ ✓

7

"I like to have the ball at my feet and I give the players in front of me calmness, knowing I'm back there trying to protect them."

POSITION: DEFENDER

VICTOR LINDELOF

2

"Victor settled in very well and, with the big games he's played already, he's only got better and gained more confidence."

JESSE LINGARD

BORN: 17 JULY 1994; VASTERAS, SWEDEN

Signed from Benfica in the summer of 2017, Victor Lindelof spent his first season in Manchester getting used to English football. Previously a Portuguese league champion, the ice-cool Swedish international grew increasingly important to the Reds' cause.

As a boy, Victor played both football and ice hockey, and he still has plenty of skills on the ice!

DID YOU KNOW?

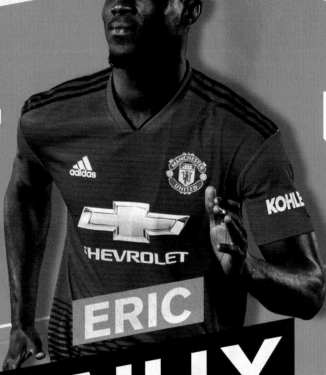

3

IN HIS OWN WORDS

"Ever since I was small I've always enjoyed the tackles. If I lose one, I'm not pleased. The tackles for me are fundamental."

ERIC
BAILLY

BORN: 12 APRIL 1994; BINGERVILLE, IVORY COAST

"He's so solid, nobody gets around him and I'm so glad that we have him here."

LUKE SHAW

BEST UNITED MOMENT (SO FAR)

Upon arriving from Villarreal in 2016, Eric Bailly quickly established himself as a fans' favourite. The Ivorian is hard as nails and a great defensive reader of the game, but also very comfortable in possession. A proper all-round modern centre-back.

After winning his first major medal with the Reds in the 2017 League Cup final, Eric capped his day with a memorable role in the trophy celebrations!

"I really enjoy reading the game from centre back. Stepping in, winning headers and setting attacks off, it suits my game."

4

POSITION: DEFENDER

PHIL JONES

BORN: 21 FEBRUARY 1992; PRESTON, ENGLAND

"I've played alongside Jonah since our England under-21 days and I've always enjoyed it. He's a top defender."

CHRIS SMALLING

One of the last signings of the Sir Alex Ferguson era, England international Phil Jones has won almost every trophy during his time at Old Trafford. A natural-born defender, he will put himself on the line and risk literally any part of his body to protect United's goal!

BEST UNITED MOMENT (SO FAR)

After losing the title with the final kick of 2011/12, getting his hands on the 2012/13 Premier League trophy was worth the wait.

"I am mostly an offensive player and I think more about attacking, going forward and helping the strikers. I like to be in front of the goals too."

6

POSITION: MIDFIELDER

PAUL

POGBA

"Paul has got the world at his feet - he can do anything he wants."

BORN: 15 MARCH 1993; LAGNY-SUR-MARNE, FRANCE

One of the best midfielders in football, French international Paul Pogba brings unbelievable technique to United's engine room. Goals, assists and slick skills are the norm for a player who is key to how the Reds perform.

BEST UNITED MOMENT (SO FAR)

Scoring twice in the Manchester derby to silence the Etihad!

7

ALEXIS

"It's a dream to play for United. I looked at the badge and my hairs just stood up on end."

POSITION: FORWARD

BORN: 19 DECEMBER 1988; TOCOPILLA, CHILE

"Alexis has brought some excellent qualities to the squad – I'm very happy he's with us and he will help us in the future."

NEMANJA MATIC

As he has shown against United in the past, Alexis can be unplayable on his day. The little Chilean has pace, power and trickery, but more importantly gives 100 per cent in every game – no surprise, then, that he can make the difference in huge matches.

DID YOU KNOW?

Alexis is such a hero in Chile, that his hometown of Tocopilla unveiled a statue of him and named a road after him!

POSITION: MIDFIELDER

8

IN HIS OWN WORDS

"I like players who make the game simple, who make it look easy even though it's not."

JUAN

KOHLER

MATA

"Probably the nicest footballer I've met, and a wonderful footballer. The things he's won in his career are a joke."

LUKE SHAW

BORN: 28 APRIL 1988; BURGOS, SPAIN

The nicest man in football? Maybe, but Juan Mata is also one of the most successful. The little Spaniard has among the sharpest brains and softest touches around, and he can cause chaos from any attacking role.

BEST UNITED MOMENT (SO FAR)

Scoring a match-winning double at Anfield takes some beating!

9

IN HIS OWN WORDS

"People in football love to talk about mental strength. Well, I'm the strongest dude you're ever going to meet."

POSITION: FORWARD

"Romelu is such a positive character. He loves to score goals, but even if he doesn't, he makes sure that he gives everything for the team."

JUAN MATA

ROMELU
LUKAKU

BORN: 13 MAY 1993; ANTWERP, BELGIUM

Belgium's all-time top goalscorer, one of United's biggest-ever signings and one of the most unstoppable strikers in the game. As well as being a man-mountain, Romelu Lukaku is also psychologically as sharp as they come. Good luck, defenders!

DID YOU KNOW?

Lukaku made his first senior appearance 11 days after his 16th birthday, as a substitute for Anderlecht in the Belgian cup final!

POSITION: FORWARD

10

IN HIS OWN WORDS

"I work on every type of finishing, because you have to judge in the moment what sort of finish is needed to score."

MARCUS

RASHFORD

BORN: 31 OCTOBER 1997; MANCHESTER, ENGLAND

"He has a lot of qualities and, for me, he is maybe the most complete No. 9. He can do everything."

ROMELU LUKAKU

An electric young talent who came from nowhere to suddenly become a fixture in United's squad, Marcus Rashford is one of the game's best goalscoring prospects. He's also an Academy product and a boyhood Red. Top Manc.

DID YOU KNOW?

Less than 24 hours after scoring twice on his Premier League debut against Arsenal as an 18-year-old, Marcus had to go into school the next morning!

11

"I love Manchester United. I love the fans. They give me a lot of joy."

POSITION: FORWARD

ANTHONY MARTIAL

BORN: 5 DECEMBER 1995; MASSY, FRANCE

"Anthony really is one of the best I've seen. He can run with the ball as if it's stuck to his foot – the only other player I've seen like that is Leo Messi."

SERGIO ROMERO

The man who inspired Martial FC to become a social media presence really does have it all. One of the most exciting young attackers anywhere in world football, Tony Martial can become as good as he wants to be.

BEST UNITED MOMENT (SO FAR)

So, you're making your United debut. Against Liverpool. And you score a ridiculous solo goal to clinch victory. Whaaat??

POSITION: DEFENDER

12

IN HIS OWN WORDS

"With or without the captain's armband it's about being that leader, being that vocal person on the pitch."

CHRIS
SMALLING

BORN: 22 NOVEMBER 1989; GREENWICH, ENGLAND

"He will play every game and be strong for you. He's popped up with some really important goals along the way for us as well."

JESSE LINGARD

One of the Reds' most experienced defenders, Chris Smalling has won almost every available honour since joining United in 2010. A fine athletic specimen and a natural-born defender who loves to grapple with opposing strikers.

BEST UNITED MOMENT (SO FAR)

Ending his first campaign at Old Trafford as a Premier League champion, just a couple of years after playing non-league football!

13

IN HIS OWN WORDS

"It's a mammoth task ahead to try to dislodge the other keepers, but I'm really looking forward to learning off them and working with them."

POSITION: GOALKEEPER

"Lee has great experience and he's more than ready to fulfil the role we want."

JOSE MOURINHO

LEE GRANT

BORN: 27 JANUARY 1983; HEMEL HEMPSTEAD, ENGLAND

Lee Grant is proof that good things come to those who wait. The former England youth international spent time with various clubs in the Championship before making his Premier League debut with Stoke in 2016 at 33. His form with the Potters included a man-of-the-match display to frustrate United at Old Trafford, convincing the Reds to sign him up as experienced cover.

DID YOU KNOW?

At Derby County, Lee worked with former Reds goalkeeping coach Eric Steele, the man who advised United to sign David De Gea back in 2011!

POSITION: FORWARD

14

JESSE LINGARD

"He's always been a top player and the movements that he makes off the ball are terrific. Now he's getting the final thing – whether it's a goal or an assist – and things have come together for him."

MARCUS RASHFORD

BORN: 15 DECEMBER 1992; WARRINGTON, ENGLAND

Now you see him, now you don't. Jesse Lingard is the master of movement in United's attack, popping up from deep positions to net all sorts of slick finishes. Not only does he have the skills, he has the moves to celebrate too.

BEST UNITED MOMENT (SO FAR)

Scoring the winning goal in the 2016 FA Cup final win over Crystal Palace. An absolute scorcher from the homegrown hero. What a moment!

15

"I had a lot of experiences out on loan and I am very happy to be back. I want to show that I am ready to play for United."

POSITION: MIDFIELDER

ANDREAS
PEREIRA

"He is my brother from another mother and I hope for the best for him. I hope he wins many trophies and I am sure he will succeed well at this big club."

JOEL PEREIRA

BORN: 1 JANUARY 1996; DUFFEL, BELGIUM

BRAZIL INTERNATIONAL

Though he spent 2016/17 and 2017/18 out on loan in **Spain** with Granada and Valencia, Andreas Pereira still has his heart set on a big impact at **Old Trafford**. The Belgium-born Brazilian starlet is a superb midfield string-puller who can play in a wide variety of positions and is itching for a chance to show it with the Reds.

BEST UNITED MOMENT (SO FAR)

Andreas displayed his sensational free-kick technique in a League Cup win over Ipswich Town with a stunning set-piece into the top corner. Pick that one out!

POSITION: DEFENDER

IN HIS OWN WORDS

"I like to compete. I prefer making a goal-saving tackle or a block to scoring a goal."

MARCOS
ROJO

CHEVROLET

KOHLE

BORN: 20 MARCH 1990; LA PLATA, ARGENTINA

"I have told Marcos that he's in the top five central defenders in the world."

ANDER HERRERA

A tough-tackling, versatile defender who can play in central defence or at left-back, the Argentina international has featured for his country at the last two World Cups. In true Argentinian tradition, he's as hard as they come – don't mess with Marcos!

BEST UNITED MOMENT (SO FAR)

May 2016 – Lifting the FA Cup in just his second season at the club

17

POSITION: MIDFIELDER

IN HIS OWN WORDS

"When I was young, Manchester United was a name I used to hear or see on computer games and I used to play with the team. For me, Manchester United means greatness."

FRED

CHEVROLET

KOHL

BORN: 5 MARCH 1993; BELO HORIZONTE, BRAZIL

"He is the kind of player we need to complement the qualities of our other midfield players."

JOSE
MOURINHO

Five years with Shakhtar Donetsk in Ukraine yielded three league titles and another seven winner's medals in the country's cup competitions for Fred, the Brazilian international charged with bringing energy and incision to United's midfield. His intelligence and forward-thinking were key reasons for his signing, and he is expected to bring much-needed balance to the Reds' engine room over the coming years.

DID YOU KNOW?

Fred faced United at Old Trafford during his first season with Shakhtar, starring in a tight Champions League game which was settled by a single goal from Phil Jones.

IN HIS OWN WORDS

"There's a lot said now about younger players that it's just about the cars and houses. I'm from the old school – it's about what you've achieved in the game."

18

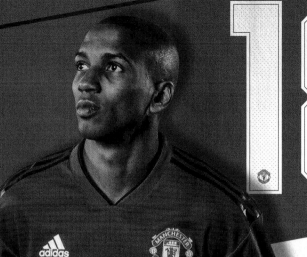

ASHLEY YOUNG

BORN: 9 JULY 1985; STEVENAGE, ENGLAND

"He's adapted well to playing full-back. I think he's a natural leader at the back for us. He always plays with 100% passion."

JESSE LINGARD

An international level attacker for the majority of his career, Ashley Young reinvented himself as a full-back in his 30s and became a defensive starter for both United and England. A proper pro, but also one of the heads of the dressing room.

BEST UNITED MOMENT (SO FAR)

Easy. Winning the 2012/13 Premier League in his second season at Old Trafford – something he's always happy to remind young pretenders about!

20

IN HIS OWN WORDS

"I'm very instant in improving and I'm mostly a hard-working player. I prefer to play at right-back, but if I need to play in any position, I will play, no problem."

POSITION: DEFENDER

DIOGO
DALOT

"In his age group, he is the best full-back in Europe."

JOSE MOURINHO

BORN: 18 MARCH 1999; BRAGA, PORTUGAL

The Reds' first signing of the 2018 summer transfer window was an unexpected one, but **Jose Mourinho** moved quickly to secure a player who had made a big impression in his early months in Porto's first team. Diogo quickly established himself as a hot prospect for the future with his versatility, commitment and reading of the game, prompting his huge move to Old Trafford!

DID YOU KNOW?

While he had never played in English football before joining United, Diogo had sampled Anfield after helping Porto keep a Champions League clean sheet against Liverpool.

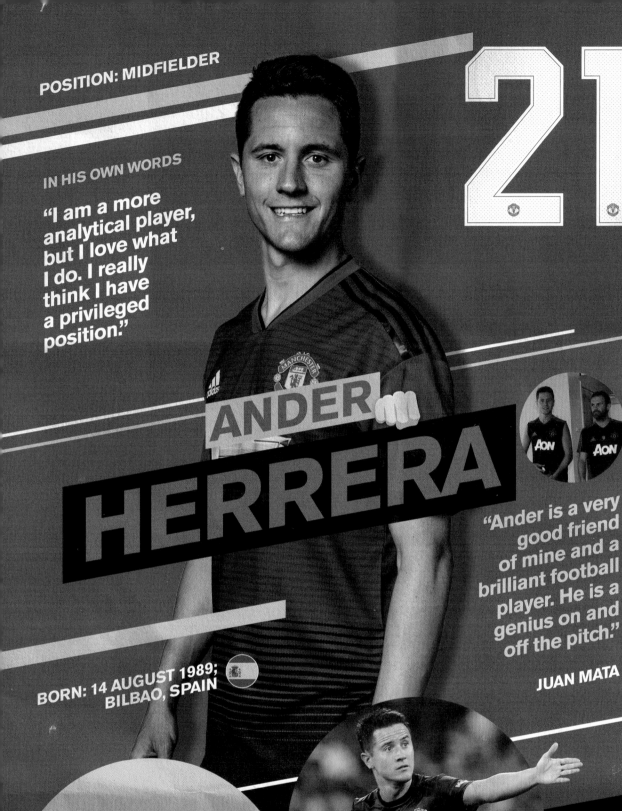

POSITION: MIDFIELDER

21

IN HIS OWN WORDS

"I am a more analytical player, but I love what I do. I really think I have a privileged position."

ANDER
HERRERA

"Ander is a very good friend of mine and a brilliant football player. He is a genius on and off the pitch."

JUAN MATA

BORN: 14 AUGUST 1989; BILBAO, SPAIN

A non-stop dynamo in United's midfield, Ander Herrera has given his all since his 2014 arrival at Old Trafford. Another versatile player who can operate either in a withdrawn role or up in support of the attackers, he can also execute man-marking jobs to brilliant effect. A top player and a real dressing room joker.

DID YOU KNOW?

Ander's father used to be a scout and general manager for Real Zaragoza. When Ander was seven years old, he used to watch matches and tell his Dad which players to sign!

22

POSITION: GOALKEEPER

SERGIO
ROMERO

"Sergio has all his experience, particularly with the Argentinian national team, and his standards are always excellent, always very high."

DAVID DE GEA

BORN: 22 FEBRUARY 1987; BERNARDO DE IRIGOYEN, ARGENTINA

Despite competing with **David De Gea**, Sergio Romero has enjoyed a hugely successful United career. He has played his part in the team winning three major honours, while his individual record for notching clean sheets is beyond a joke. In his first three seasons at the club, he notched 23 shutouts in 37 games!

BEST UNITED MOMENT (SO FAR)

Rounding off a superb Europa League campaign with a vital clean sheet against Ajax in the final, then picking up the much-deserved trophy. Vamos!

POSITION: DEFENDER

23

IN HIS OWN WORDS

"I'm always proud and happy to help the team. I try to make my family proud and I always want to be the first name on the teamsheet."

LUKE
SHAW

BORN: 12 JULY 1995; KINGSTON-UPON-THAMES, ENGLAND

"Luke is super quick, super strong, technically very good and he can put in some good crosses when he gets forward."

PHIL JONES

Luke Shaw has had to be patient since joining United from Southampton in 2014, but he is still one of the most exciting young defensive talents around. Whether he's playing at full-back or wing-back, the England defender has absolutely devastating pace and a variety of skills that most defenders can only dream of.

BEST UNITED MOMENT (SO FAR)

On his 67th appearance for United, Luke netted the first goal of his senior career against Leicester in August 2018. As his celebrations showed, he was made up!

25

ANTONIO VALENCIA

IN HIS OWN WORDS

"My time at Manchester United has been like a dream come true for me – all I can do is give everything I have for this huge, great club, my team-mates and the supporters."

POSITION: DEFENDER

BORN: 4 AUGUST 1985; LAGO AGRIO, ECUADOR

"There's just one word for Antonio: machine! The guy is just a machine!"

PHIL JONES

Installed as United's new club captain following the retirement of Michael Carrick, Antonio Valencia has come a long way from his early years in Ecuador! Signed as a flying right winger back in 2009, Tony is now recognised as one of the best right-backs around and a model of consistency who leads by example in the dressing room.

BEST UNITED MOMENT (SO FAR)

Though captaining United to Europa League glory was a huge personal honour, Antonio has always spoken of his pride at being the first Ecuadorian to lift the Premier League trophy.

POSITION: MIDFIELDER

27

IN HIS OWN WORDS

"I am very happy at Manchester United, I have enjoyed my journey here and I feel like we have a lot we still want to achieve together."

MAROUANE FELLAINI

"Felli always trains right and plays right as well. Just the presence of him means he can score goals, and he's popped up with some really important ones for us down the years."

JESSE LINGARD

BORN: 22 NOVEMBER 1987; ETTERBEEK, BELGIUM

Trusted on the big occasions by every United manager he has worked with, Marouane Fellaini is a unique midfield talent. The lofty Belgian has made key contributions for both his club and country in recent years – including a big role in Belgium's third-place finish at the 2018 World Cup – and his commitment to a new contract ahead of 2018/19 was a huge boost for the Reds.

BEST UNITED MOMENT (SO FAR)

A key goal in the 2016 FA Cup semi-final, made all the sweeter because it came against his former club, Everton!

29

31

IN HIS OWN WORDS

"In my position, the player needs to give balance to the team and control the game and that is what I try to do. You have to know every time where the ball is."

POSITION: MIDFIELDER

NEMANJA
MATIC

"I always knew he was a good player but coming up close to him in training and seeing how he's performed with us, it's gone to a whole new level of appreciation."

CHRIS SMALLING

BORN: 1 AUGUST 1988; ŠABAC, SERBIA

Nemanja Matic's 2017 arrival at Old Trafford was the third time he had been signed by Jose Mourinho, underlining just how highly the Portuguese thinks of the Serbian midfielder. An expert reader of the game and destroyer of opposing attacks, Nemanja also has the ability to crack home some stunning long-range goals.

DID YOU KNOW?

Nemanja isn't just a football player – he owns two entire clubs back in his native Serbia!

POSITION: DEFENDER

36

IN HIS OWN WORDS

"I have almost always been a defender and, as a defender and playing in the youth team for AC Milan, my idols were always Paolo Maldini and Alessandro Nesta."

MATTEO
DARMIAN

"It's always good to have players that can play in various positions in a team. Wherever he plays, Matteo performs the role well and we can trust him to play in that position."

JESSE LINGARD

BORN: 2 DECEMBER 1989; LEGNANO, ITALY

Bought from Torino in 2015, Italian international Matteo Darmian quickly slotted in on the right side of United's defence. In the ensuing three seasons, the dependable former AC Milan defender occasionally switched flanks to the left side and invariably put in a solid shift wherever he was asked to play. A true professional.

BEST UNITED MOMENT (SO FAR)

Matteo was absolutely outstanding against Ajax in the 2017 Europa League final, turning in a flawless display as the Reds completed the club's set of major trophies.

39

IN HIS OWN WORDS

"Brought up playing for Manchester United, whether it's playing for the U10s when you're a little kid – which is the best thing in the world – or whether it's playing in the first team, you feel incredible every time you play for the club."

POSITION: MIDFIELDER

SCOTT
MCTOMINAY

"It's hard to break through the Academy at United, but he's broken through and done very well. He plays for the shirt and that's all we can ask from him."

JESSE LINGARD

BORN: 8 DECEMBER 1996; LANCASTER, ENGLAND

SCOTLAND INTERNATIONAL

One of the youth system's big surprises of recent years, Scott McTominay was a late developer who suddenly burst to prominence at the highest level when Jose Mourinho gave him a breakthrough. Like all top players, Scott took the opportunity with both hands and showed his ability to compete in midfield at the highest level.

BEST UNITED MOMENT (SO FAR)

The Scotland international completely shut down Chelsea star Eden Hazard during a must-win Premier League meeting at Old Trafford in 2017/18.

POSITION: FORWARD

44

IN HIS OWN WORDS

IN HIS OWN WORDS

"After my injury, I'm just enjoying football and will keep working hard. Character is important and I've just got to keep working hard and doing my job."

TAHITH CHONG

NETHERLANDS YOUTH INTERNATIONAL

BORN: 4 DECEMBER 1999; WILLEMSTAD, CURACAO

"The talent is there, the personality is there, the passion, the desire to play, the humility to learn. Technically he's very good, tactically he understands the game. He understands his position."

JOSE MOURINHO

Rated as one of the hottest young prospects in Dutch football, Tahith joined United from Feyenoord in 2016. Even though he suffered a serious knee injury and missed 10 months of action, his subsequent form not only earned him the Jimmy Murphy Young Player of the Year award in 2018, it also earned him a spot on the seniors' pre-season tour.

DID YOU KNOW?

When he had to perform his initiation song in front of the first team squad, Tahith opted for Michael Jackson's 'Man in the Mirror' – and he smashed it!

33

46

JOSHUA BOHUI

"We want to attract the best young players around and bring them into what we feel is already a great setup – Josh fell into that category."

NICKY BUTT

BORN: 3 MARCH 1999; LONDON, ENGLAND

A 2016 arrival at Old Trafford, Joshua left Brentford's youth system to take a place at United, and his rapid attacking play gave him the ability to make the step up in standards. His goalscoring form in the UEFA Youth League showed that he can cut it at the highest level, and his displays in the youth ranks prompted his inclusion in the first team's 2018 pre-season squad.

DID YOU KNOW?

Though he has represented England at youth level, Joshua is still eligible to represent Ivory Coast and France because of his Ivorian father.

POSITION: MIDFIELDER

47

IN HIS OWN WORDS

IN HIS OWN WORDS

"Winning titles is huge for me. I want to play international football, play in World Cups and European Championships. I want to be the best player at my age level. I set myself high standards and try to push myself to play at the highest level."

ANGEL
GOMES

CHEVROLET

"He's small, but his feet are so fast; the fastest in the Academy! He's one of the best I've ever seen on the ball!"

CLAYTON BLACKMORE

BORN: 31 AUGUST 2000; LONDON, ENGLAND

One of the most exciting young talents in the country, Angel made his first team debut for the Reds at the age of just 16. Though his 2017/18 campaign was heavily disrupted by injuries, his form since returning has demonstrated his huge gifts. Sharp, intelligent and brilliantly balanced in his attacking play, he also has a cool head under pressure and has massive potential.

DID YOU KNOW?

Angel was the first player in Premier League history to have been born in the 21st century!

35

48

"It's amazing to see all the senior guys around the training ground, look at what they do, how they act around the place – and try to emulate it. I try to take bits of information from all of them."

POSITION: MIDFIELDER

ETHAN HAMILTON

"With his attitude, it could certainly carry him very far in his career."

KIERAN MCKENNA

BORN: 18 OCTOBER 1998; EDINBURGH, SCOTLAND

Another to make the cut for United's 2018 pre-season tour, Ethan is a non-stop, box-to-box midfielder who has boundless energy and enthusiasm. The Scottish youth international gives his all for the Reds, and his committed displays in the youth ranks have already resulted in first team recognition, with a spot on the first team bench during 2017/18.

DID YOU KNOW?

Ethan graduated from Hutchison Vale, the same Edinburgh youth team as former Reds and Scotland midfielder Darren Fletcher, who looked after him during their time together at Old Trafford.

51

IN HIS OWN WORDS

"I always try to show the best I can. Every day since I came to United I've been training hard. Chances have come to me and I think I've taken them."

MATEJ
KOVAR

"He looks a really talented goalkeeper. He has a great physique, is good with his feet and he's a lovely lad as well who speaks good English."

KIERAN McKENNA

CHEVROLET

KOHLER

BORN: 17 MAY 2000; UHERSKÉ HRADIŠTĚ, CZECH REPUBLIC

After impressing United's scouting network, Czech Republic youth international Matej was handed a trial at the Aon Training Complex and he took his chance with both hands. He was given a permanent deal on transfer deadline day in January 2018 and quickly slotted into the youth setup, where his calm, composed displays have already pushed him into senior squad contention.

DID YOU KNOW?

One of Matej's mentors is Ludek Miklosko, who repeatedly came up against United as West Ham's goalkeeper during the 1990s.

MOVE LIKE
JLINGZ!

Academy lad Jesse Lingard loves scoring for United – just look at his array of celebrations!

DABBING

When the hip-hop move made it into the mainstream in 2015, Jesse used it at St James' Park after scoring against Newcastle!

SHOUTOUTS TO DRAKE…

As a fan of the Canadian rapper (in this instance the song 'Portland'), JLingz aired this flute-playing jig as a tribute after goals at Middlesbrough and Swansea.

…AND YOUNG THUG

"I feel like I'm Hercules," tweeted Jesse after his superb goal at Watford, where his celebration nodded to a line in rapper Young Thug's song 'Mink Flow'.

MILLY ROCK

With another hip-hop reference, this time JLingz rocked the Emirates Stadium by busting out 2 Milly's 'Milly Rock' after netting against Arsenal.

WAKANDA FOREVER

Not just limited by musical references, Jesse whipped out his best Black Panther impersonation after heading home the winner against Chelsea!

GOING SOLO

Shelving the dance moves, Lingard now has his very own celebration, forming the initials 'JL' with his hands in a move he calls 'JLingz'.

TEAM EFFORT

Of course, Jesse's more than happy to let his mates get in on the act too!

5 REASONS
DE GEA IS THE WORLD'S
NO.1 GOALKEEPER!

HE MAKES THE IMPOSSIBLE POSSIBLE

There is no human explanation for some of the saves David makes. Even when opponents hammer shots at him from point-blank range, he can block them. If they're going right in the top bin, he can flick them away. If a striker goes through on goal, he can read their mind and deny them a goal. There's no other goalie in the world who can make his range of unbelievable stops.

HE CAN IMPROVISE LIKE NOBODY ELSE

David's been at it for years, but just look back to 2017/18 for glaring examples of him making saves that nobody else would even think to make. His big toe stopped Joel Matip scoring for Liverpool at Anfield, then Alexis Sanchez in our win over Arsenal at the Emirates Stadium. That kind of quick-thinking is one major asset which sets Dave apart from the rest.

HE'S GOT BALL SKILLS

It's super fashionable to have a ball-playing goalkeeper in the Premier League these days, and David's a veteran in that sense. From his first day at Old Trafford, the Spaniard has been one of the very best around with the ball at his feet, whether he's fielding short passes or pinging long ones forward to launch attacks.

HE NEEDS A NEW AWARDS CABINET

No player has won the Sir Matt Busby Player of the Year trophy more times than De Gea. Not Ronaldo, not Rooney, not Giggs... you get the picture. Consider this, too: in his first seven seasons in England, he's been in the PFA Team of the Year five times and won Match of the Day's Save of the Season five times. Five!

HE'S GETTING EVEN BETTER!

David has steadily improved every single season since he moved to Old Trafford in 2011. Going into 2018/19, De Gea is 27 years old, which, for a goalkeeper, is still very young. For context, Peter Schmeichel was 27 when he signed for United, and Edwin van der Sar was 34. There is no limit to how good Dave can become.

RED TO 💯 THE CORE

United's youth system is rightly world famous. The Reds have had an Academy graduate in every single matchday squad dating back to October 1937. That's almost 4,000 consecutive games! From the Busby Babes to the Class of '92, some truly great talents have risen through the Reds' Academy to make it to the first team. Here, some of the current squad's homegrown heroes talk about their own journeys through the ranks…

"It's like one big family here. Even though Jesse is four or five years older than me, he's one of my best friends. When you are at U11s and U16s everyone is mingling together and you share the same canteen and whatever you do, everyone does it together. That's the biggest thing that sticks with you. Everyone is like a family and we all fight for each other."

MARCUS RASHFORD

"Since I've played in a lot of different positions in the Academy, it has made me a versatile player. I can play anywhere on the pitch and that helps me a lot."

ANDREAS PEREIRA

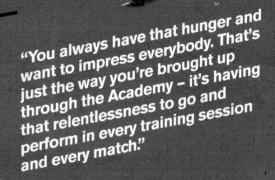

"I love the club. I came in the Academy, I grew up, I played for the first team. For me, it was a dream come true. It's even more because of the past, because of the players that played here."

PAUL POGBA

SCOTT MCTOMINAY

"You always have that hunger and want to impress everybody. That's just the way you're brought up through the Academy – it's having that relentlessness to go and perform in every training session and every match."

"It's great to be recognised as a homegrown player coming through the ranks and making it to the first team; we can only thank the staff that have helped us along the way. If we can win trophies together over a lot of seasons then that would be perfect."

JESSE LINGARD

MANCHESTER UNITED
WOMEN

OUR
TIME
IS
NOW

2018/19 is a historic season: the first-ever campaign of a professional Manchester United Women's team. Meet the gaffer and her players...

"I truly believe that Manchester United has the ability to change the face of women's football forever. The players are excited, the women's game is excited and it's a massive journey to go on, but an exciting one."

CASEY
STONEY

"I see it as a challenge. For me it's an opportunity to form something, to create something, to mould a team your own way, to get the players in, coach them, work with them and create something from scratch – it is really exciting."

"My ultimate aim is to grow this team so that every little girl growing up dreams when she's older she wants to play for Manchester United, because they're the most successful team in women's football."

GOALKEEPERS

SIOBHAN
CHAMBERLAIN

1

A veteran international stopper who has passed half a century of caps for England. With a wealth of experience from World Cups, European Championships, not to mention the UEFA Women's Champions League, she brings invaluable knowhow to a fledgling team.

CASEY SAYS

"Siobhan's experience will be vital with the youthful look of our squad. A real team player and a very driven individual. The thinker of the team."

EMILY
RAMSEY

13

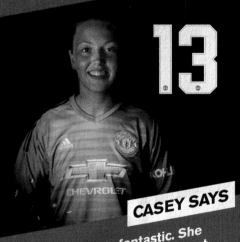

Having previously emerged through United's youth ranks before going to join Liverpool – where she worked with Reds colleague Siobhan Chamberlain – Emily is back where it all began. Already an England youth international, she is seen as a player with brimming potential.

CASEY SAYS

"To be able to bring Emily back is fantastic. She has a fantastic future ahead of her and is a great addition to our squad. Emily can achieve whatever she wants and we will support her to get there."

22

FRAN
BENTLEY

Another youth international returning for her second stint at the club – rejoining United from local rivals Manchester City – Fran couldn't be more excited to be back with her childhood club. A bright future beckons for this gifted Salfordian.

CASEY SAYS

"I'm really pleased Fran made the decision to come to United. She is a great character and has a huge amount of potential."

DEFENDERS

2

MARTHA
HARRIS

The first-ever winner of the PFA Young Player of the Year award, Martha made her name in the women's game with Liverpool, where her versatility and commitment earmarked her out as a star defender for both the present and future.

CASEY SAYS

"Martha has had some fantastic seasons at full-back and she adds real energy to our team. One of the best one v one defenders around."

ALEX
GREENWOOD

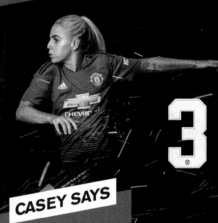

3

Named United captain upon signing, Alex guarantees a top class contribution to the Reds. An experienced full-back with Liverpool and England, she was previously named young International Player of the Year and brings savvy to the United defence.

CASEY SAYS

"Signing Alex was very significant for us. She is an experienced international and has one of the best left feet in the game, which will be vital to the way we want to play."

AMY
TURNER

An experienced defender with a blend of finesse and ferocity, Amy made her top flight debut at 16 and never looked back. Never one to shirk a challenge, she arrived at United established as one of the toughest defenders around.

4

CASEY SAYS

"Amy will drive our standards and keep the aggression on the pitch. Her ability to play out from the back was a key reason for us wanting her on board."

DEFENDERS

12

NAOMI
HARTLEY

Another youngster who learnt her trade in United's youth system, Naomi is a gritty centre-back who has already been capped by England at U17 level. Undoubtedly a talent for the future, but also for the here and now.

CASEY SAYS

"It's great to be able to bring Naomi home. She has so much potential and I can't wait to see how much we can develop her. She is strong and fearless."

15

LUCY
ROBERTS

Like many of her colleagues, Lucy is an England youth international, but she stands apart for her historical links with United. Her great, great grandad, Charlie Roberts, was the first-ever captain to lead United out at Old Trafford!

CASEY SAYS

"Lucy has lots of potential and I'm looking forward to working with her to develop her game. A very focused young woman with big aspirations."

20

KIRSTY
SMITH

A full Scotland international who spent over a decade on Hibernian's books, Kirsty is renowned in the women's game for her sensational pace and her ability to play on either side of the defence; her signing is a major coup.

CASEY SAYS

"Kirsty is a versatile full-back who can play both sides. She is very quick and will add great pace to our team. A focused and positive young woman"

MILLIE
TURNER

21

Previously captain at Bristol City, England starlet Millie brings bags of ability to the United setup. Her great technical skills made her a key recruit on the field, while her massive character ensured she would be just as influential off it.

CASEY SAYS

"The signing of Millie Turner was a big one for us. She has great ability on the ball and she can defend very well, which will complement our style of play."

MIDFIELDERS

6

AIMEE
PALMER

A youthful but mature holding midfielder, England U18 international Aimee can already set the Reds' tempo to great effect. Her broad passing range makes her a potentially key component of how United operate both defensively and offensively.

CASEY SAYS

"Aimee is mature way beyond her years. She has the ability to change a game with a pass. I'm delighted she decided on United because there is so much more to come from her."

8

MOLLIE
GREEN

A former England youth international, Mollie has built a wealth of experience with Everton after rising through the ranks across Stanley Park at Liverpool. A high-energy midfield presence, her skill on the ball made her a key addition.

CASEY SAYS

"Mollie was one of my first signings. She has great technical ability, a great character and is a really good team player. A midfielder who has the ability to change games."

MIDFIELDERS

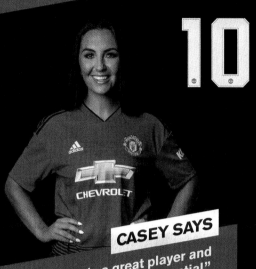

10

KATIE
ZELEM

Another graduate of the United youth system who forged a career elsewhere, Katie joins the Reds after spending a year at Juventus in Italy. There, she added further levels to her game as a powerful playmaker, and her eye for goal will be a valuable weapon in United's arsenal.

CASEY SAYS

"I'm really glad we have been able to bring Katie back. Katie is a great player and a fantastic character to have in the squad. Now we want her to reach her potential."

14

CHARLIE
DEVLIN

Blessed with quick feet and fine technical skills, Charlie is an England youth international with high level experience playing for both Arsenal and Millwall. A fine go-between for the defence and attack, her vision can unlock any opponent.

CASEY SAYS

"Charlie is a fantastic character and has lots of potential. At only 20 I can't wait to see what she can achieve. A technical midfielder who can influence games."

16

LAUREN
JAMES

The youngest member of Stoney's squad, 16-year-old Lauren has enormous potential to go far in the women's game. A technically gifted midfielder with great passing ability, she joined United after rising through Arsenal's youth system.

CASEY SAYS

"Lauren has the potential to do whatever she wants to do with hard work. She is technically very gifted and also the baby of our squad. A great addition."

FOWARDS

7

ELLA
TOONE

Like many of her colleagues, Ella is back at United after rising through the club's youth ranks and learning her trade elsewhere. Her capture from Manchester City bagged the Reds a starlet winger with the potential to make a name for herself with the Reds.

CASEY SAYS

"Ella is a great addition to the team and can play anywhere in attacking areas. She is an exciting dynamic winger and will add to our positive attacking philosophy."

9

JESS
SIGSWORTH

An England youth international, Jess was the top scorer in the Championship in 2017/18 after starring for Doncaster Belles. A true predator, she has a great eye for goal and uses her pace to devastating effect.

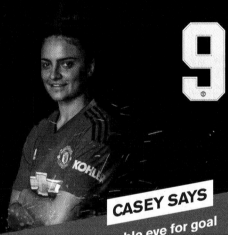

CASEY SAYS

"Jess Sigsworth knows nothing but the goal. An unbelievable eye for goal and an attitude and drive to succeed. Jess will add goals this season."

FORWARDS

LEAH
GALTON

11

Already equipped with a wealth of experience from playing in America and Germany, Leah joined United from Bayern Munich intent on making an impact with the Reds. Direct and ambitious, her left-sided trickery is a valuable asset in attack.

CASEY SAYS

"Left footers are rare and good ones even more so. Having Leah gives us really good balance and the opportunity to attack quickly on both sides. Extremely hard working and driven to take Manchester United to the next level."

17

LIZZIE
ARNOT

While a wide midfielder by trade, Scottish international Lizzie is a huge goal threat who can terrorise opponents. Dazzling with the ball at her feet, her non-stop running makes her a nightmare to play against.

CASEY SAYS

"Lizzie's energy and enthusiasm for the game is infectious. Her ability on the wing to get at the opposition will be very entertaining and exciting to watch."

KIRSTY
HANSON

18

Having represented Liverpool and Doncaster Belles, Scottish youth international Kirsty already has a wealth of key experience. An exciting wide player, blessed with pace and able to drive forward from either wing, bringing unpredictability to the Reds' attack.

19

EBONY
SALMON

Another pacey striker on United's books, Ebony is an England youth international with huge potential. Signed from Aston Villa, the teenager is seen as one of the English game's bright young attacking talents.

QUIZZES & PUZZLES

GOAL OR NO GOAL?

Take a look at these goalmouth action shots from 2017/18, then decide whether each effort resulted in a goal or not...

A

B

C

D

E

F

G

H

ANSWERS ON PAGE 60

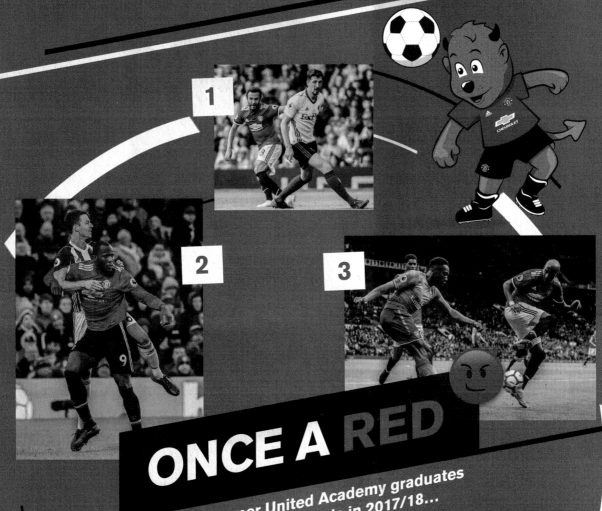

ONCE A RED

Name the former United Academy graduates playing against the Reds in 2017/18...

WORDSEARCH

FIND THE 10 HIDDEN REDS...

```
R K G I H S F A U
A U N I A A T F K
S L I N G A R D A
H N L A M E E S K
F O L E D N I L U
O A A F K X R M L
R A M L E R U N N
D M S L T O L A D
M B A I L L Y N M
```

Words go horizontally, vertically, diagonally and backwards.

ALEXIS	BAILLY	DALOT	FRED	LINDELOF
LINGARD	LUKAKU	MATA	RASHFORD	SMALLING

ANSWERS ON PAGE 60

SPOT THE DIFFERENCE

SCOUR THESE TWO PICTURES AND SEE IF YOU CAN SPOT THE SIX DIFFERENCES OUR DESIGNER HAS MADE...

ANSWERS ON PAGE 61

GIVE 'EM THE EYES!

Can you identify all 10 United players, simply by looking at these cropped pics?

JUMBLED REDS

Solve these anagrams to reveal the names of 10 legendary ex-Reds from the Premier League era

1. ALP SLOUCHES
2. LIVELY ANGER
3. NEAR YOKE
4. CONDITIONAL ROARS
5. DORKY WEIGHT
6. ADVENTUROUSLY IRON
7. PROVEN SIBERIAN
8. OCEANIC RANT
9. ANDROID FINER
10. CREATIVE RAP

SPOT THE BALL

Which of these balls has Paul Pogba just Kicked?

QUIZ ANSWERS

GOAL OR NO GOAL? PAGE 54

PIC A: NO GOAL
PIC B: NO GOAL
PIC C: GOAL
PIC D: NO GOAL
PIC E: GOAL
PIC F: GOAL
PIC G: GOAL
PIC H: GOAL

ONCE A RED   PAGE 55

1. CRAIG CATHCART
2. JONNY EVANS
3. DANNY WELBECK
4. DARREN FLETCHER
5. MICHAEL KEANE
6. JOSHUA KING
7. DANNY DRINKWATER

WORDSEARCH PAGE 56

R K G I H S F A U
A U N I A A T F K
S L I N G A R D A
H N L A M E E S K
F O L E D N I L U
O A A F K X R M L
R A M L E R U N N
D M S L T O L A D
M B A I L L Y N M

SPOT THE DIFFERENCE **PAGE 57**

SPOT THE BALL **PAGE 59**

COMPETITION

To be in with a chance of winning a 2018/19 Manchester United shirt signed by first team squad members, simply answer one easy question about the Reds...